# The Gardens

## OF THOMAS KINKADE

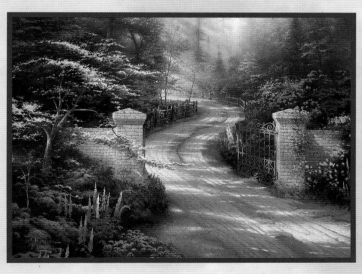

# THOMAS KINKADE

*Painter of Light*™

He leads me beside still waters


PSALMS 23

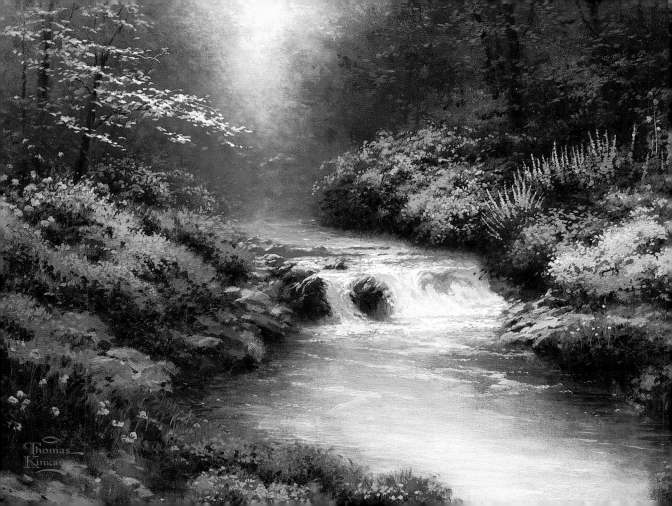

Nothing is better than simplicity

AUTHOR UNKNOWN

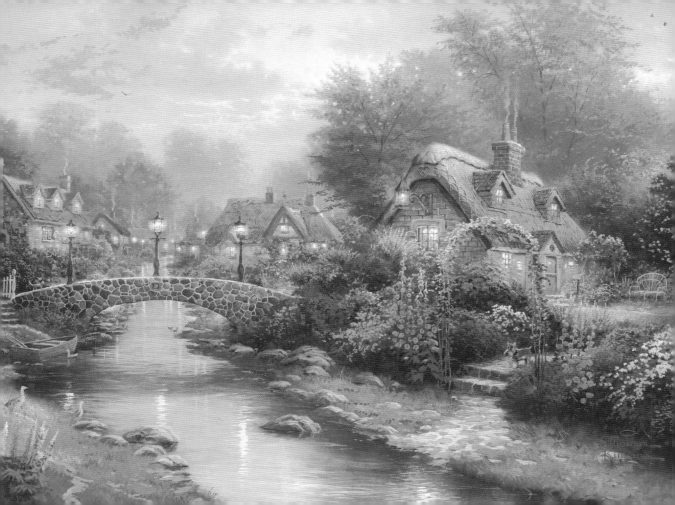

Full many a glorious morning have I seen,
flatter the mountain-tops with sovereign
eye, kissing with golden face
the meadows green, gilding pale streams
with heavenly alchemy

SHAKESPEARE

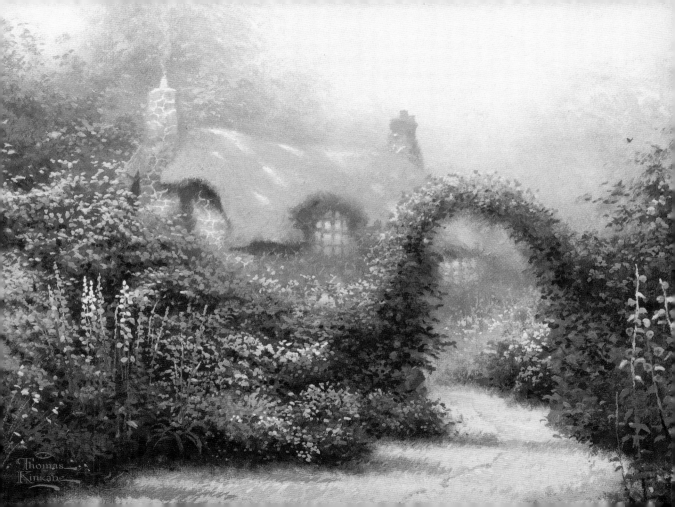

How we treat our families,
how we spend time with them,
has eternal implications

THOMAS KINKADE

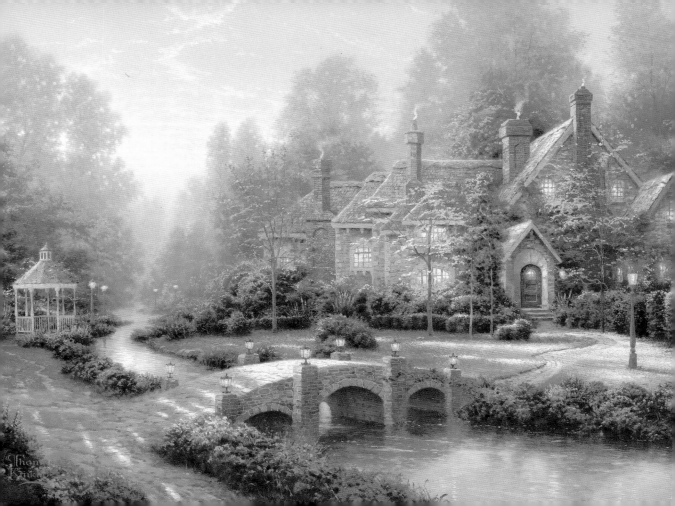

A thing of beauty is a joy forever

JOHN KEATS

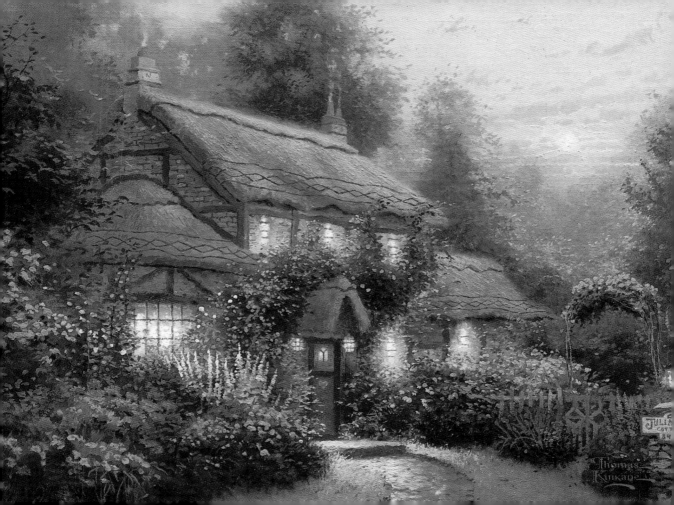

A man is content if he can find
happiness in simple pleasures

THOMAS MALLOY

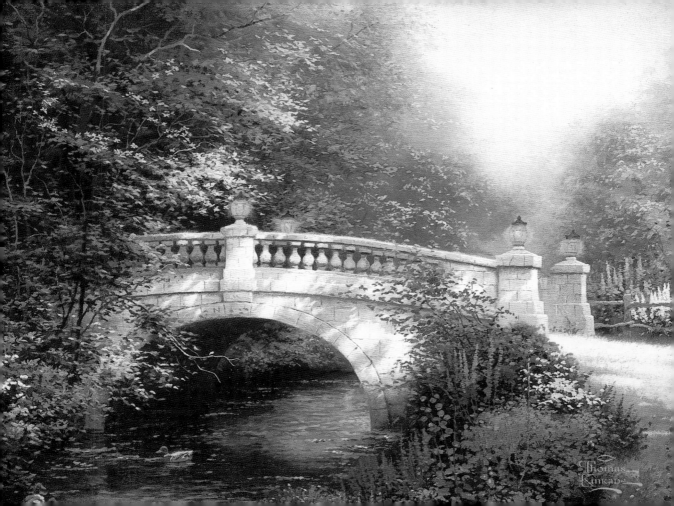

*We can do not great things;*
*only small things with great love*

MOTHER TERESA

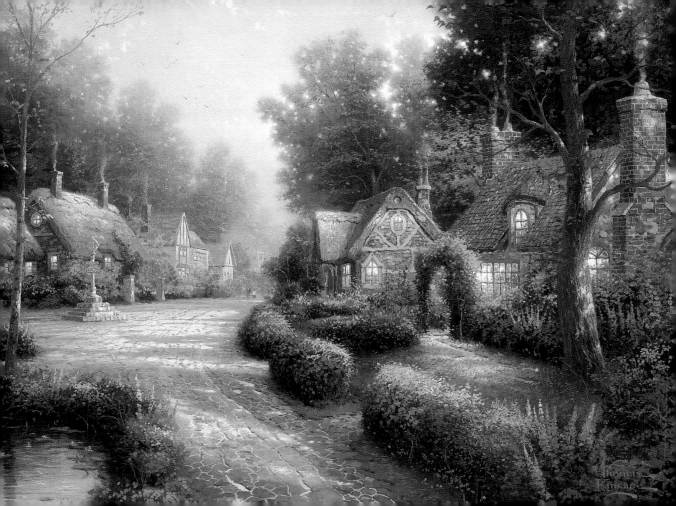

Flowers are lovely; love is flowerlike;
Friendship is a sheltering tree

SAMUEL TAYLOR COLERIDGE

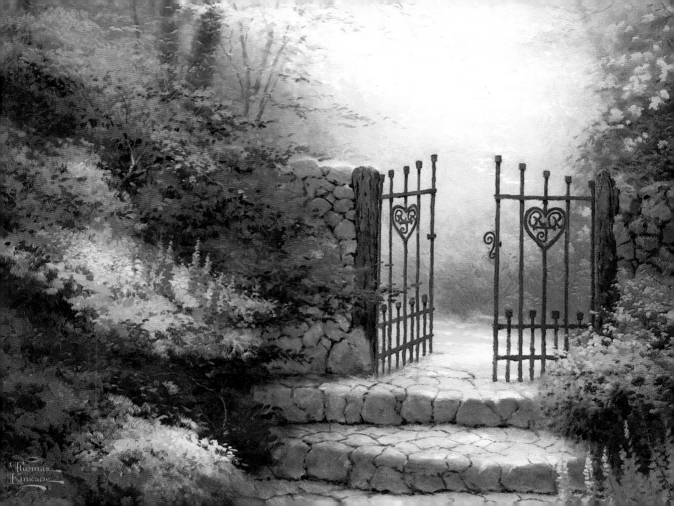

The manner of giving
is worth more than the gift

PIERRE CORNEILLE

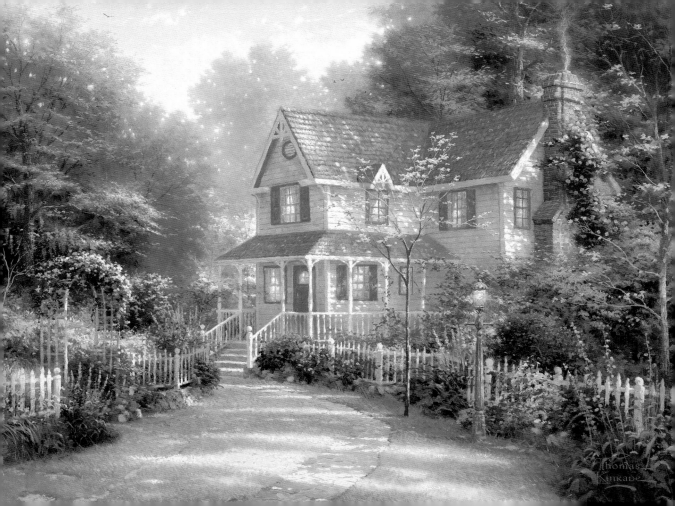

It is always sunrise somewhere

JOHN MUIR

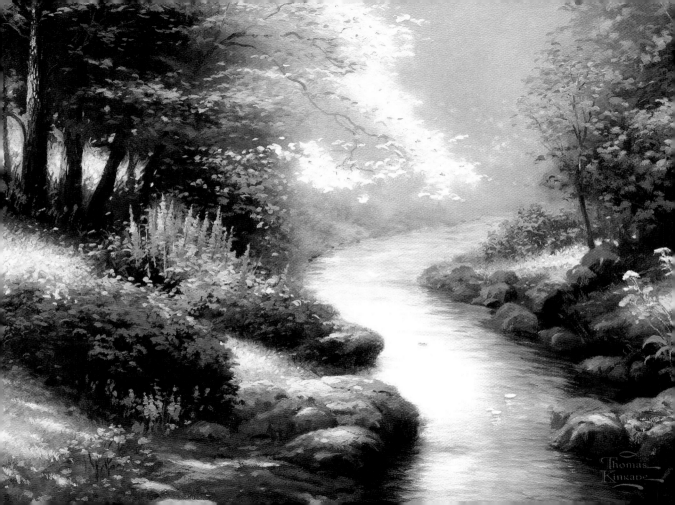

One is nearer God's heart in a garden
than anywhere else on earth

DOROTHY FRANCES GURNEY

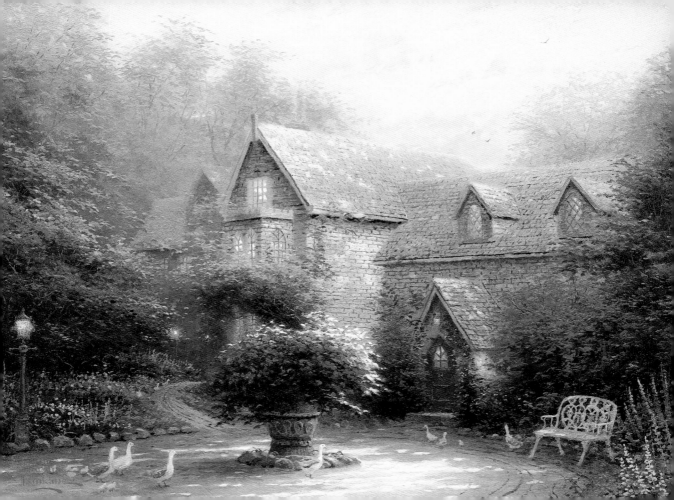

Come my beloved,
let us go to the countryside

SONG OF SOLOMON 7:11

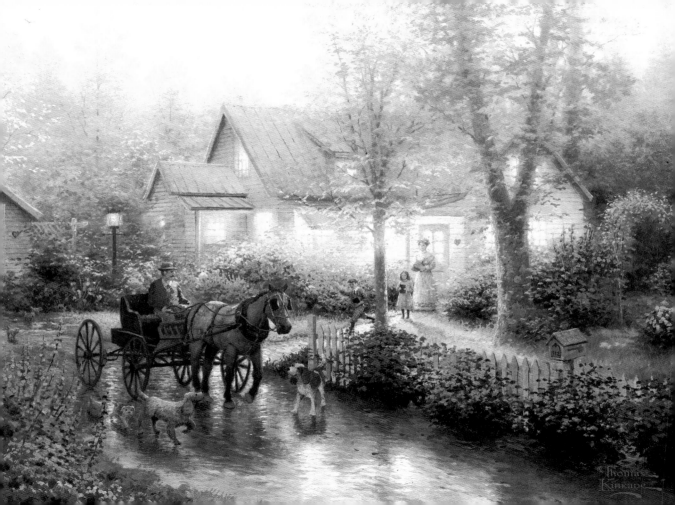

Happy is the house that shelters a friend

EMERSON

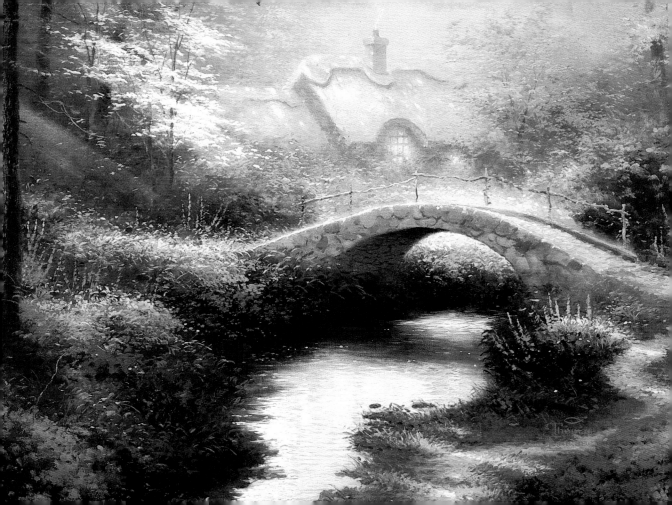

Radiate friendship
and it will be returned tenfold

HENRY P. DAVIDSON

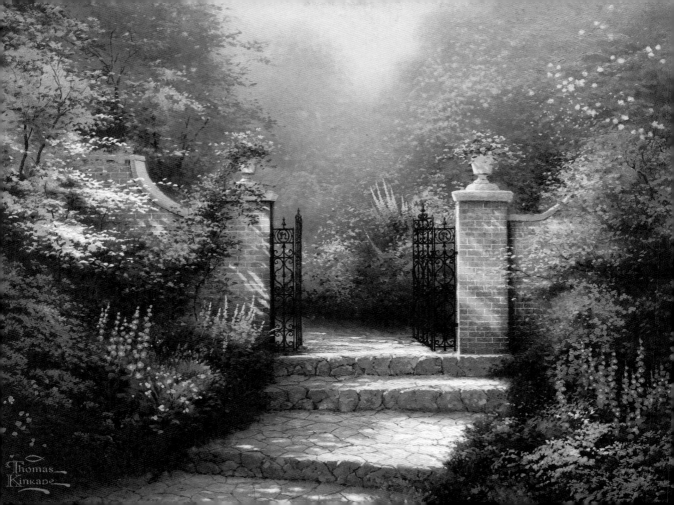

Love doesn't grow on trees like
the apples in Eden – it's something you
have to make.  And you must use
your imagination

JOYCE CARY

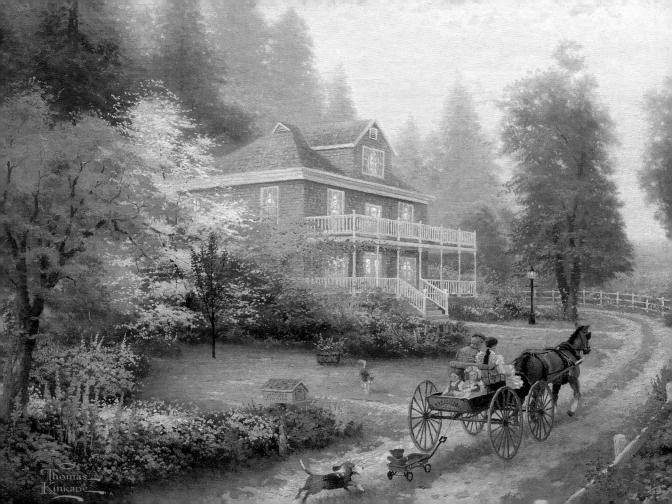

The path of love and the path
of insight lead into the same garden

STEPHEN MITCHELL

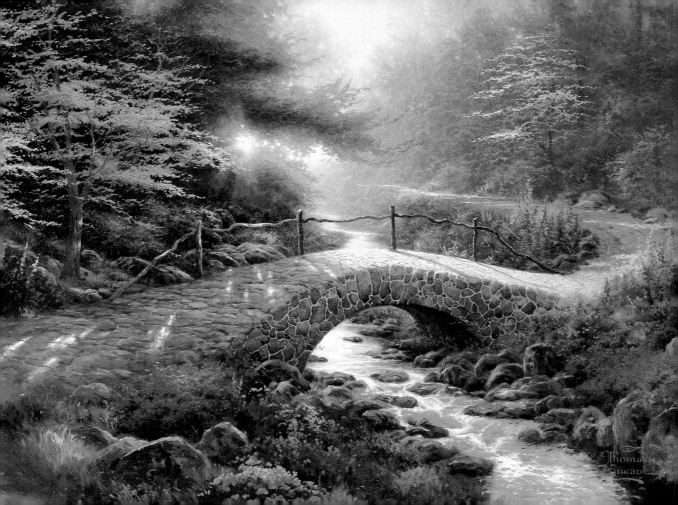

Let me live in my house by the side
of the road and be a friend to man

SAM WALTER FOSS

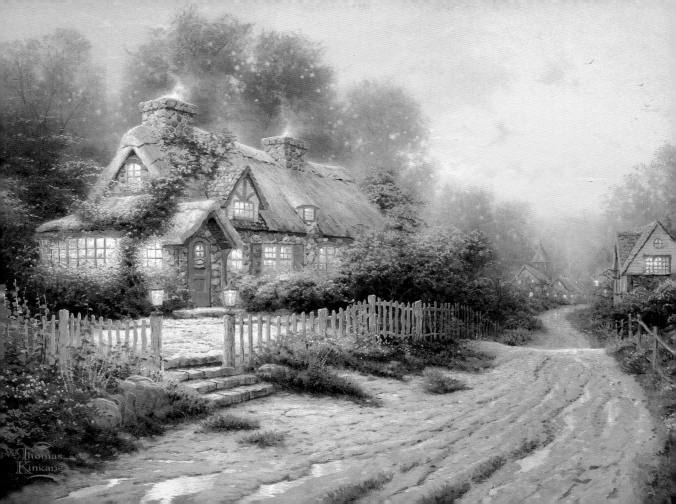

All the seasons run their race
in this quiet resting place

AUSTIN DOBSON

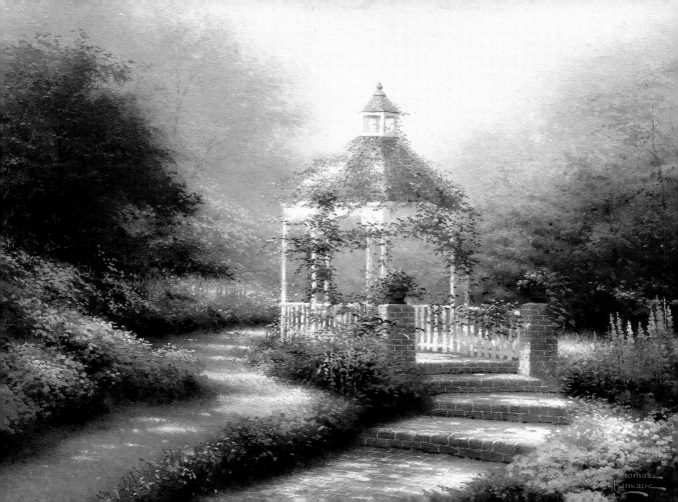

I pushed the gate that swings so silently,
and I was in the garden and aware of early
daylight on the flowers there and cups of
dew sun-kindled

AUTHOR UNKNOWN

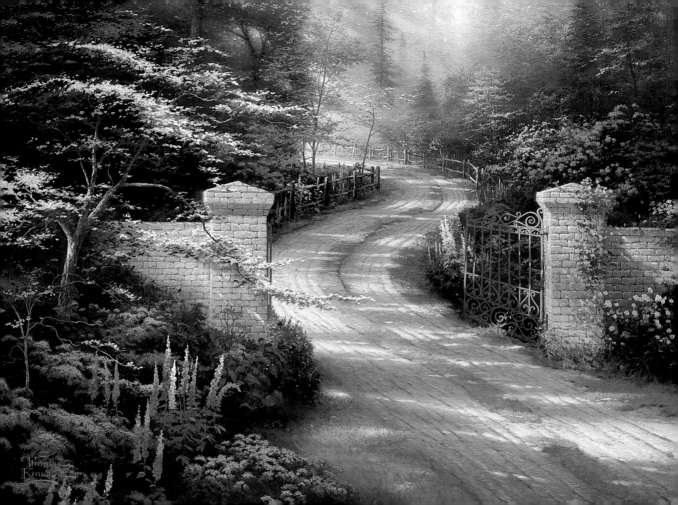

Happiness grows at our own fireside
and is not to be picked
in strangers' gardens

DOUGLAS JERROLD

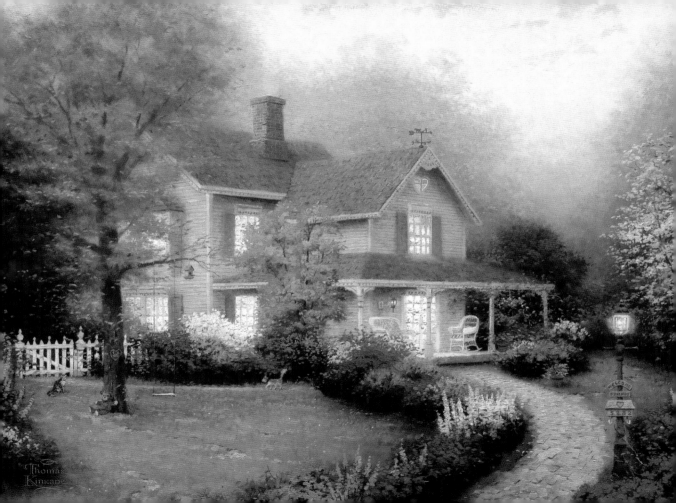

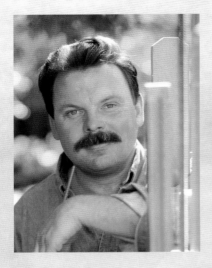

Thomas Kinkade, "The Painter of Light", is one of America's most collected artists. In the tradition of the 19th century American Luminists, Kinkade uses light to create romantic worlds that invite us in and evoke a sense of peace. Kinkade paints a wide variety of subjects, including cozy cottages, rustic outdoor scenes, dramatic landscapes, and bustling cities. Each painting radiates with the "Kinkade glow" that he attributes to "soft edges, a warm palette, and an overall sense of light."

Thomas Kinkade is a messenger of simplicity and serenity in these fast-paced turbulent times. His paintings are more than art, they are silent messengers of hope and peace that lift our spirits and touch our hearts.

Thomas Kinkade was born in Sacramento, California in 1958, raised in humble surroundings in the nearby town of Placerville. Kinkade apprenticed under Glen Wessels, an influential artist who had retired in the community. He later attended the University of California and received formal training at Art Center College of Design in Pasadena.

As a young man, Thomas Kinkade earned his living as a painter, selling his originals in galleries around California. He married his childhood sweetheart, Nanette, in 1982, and two years later they began to publish his art. In 1989 Lightpost Publishing was formed.

Thomas Kinkade is a devout Christian and credits the Lord for both the ability and the inspiration to create his paintings. His goal as an artist is to touch people of all faiths, to bring peace and joy into their lives through the images he creates. The letters he receives everyday testify to the fact that he is, at least at some level, achieving this goal.

A devoted husband and doting father to their four little girls, Kinkade always hides the letter "N" in his paintings to pay tribute to his wife, Nanette, and the girls often find their names and images tucked into the corners of his works.

*"As an artist I create paintings that bring to life my inspirational thoughts and feelings of love, family and faith. I hope each image in my collection acts as a messenger of hope, joy and peace to you and your family."*

# Welcome to the Thomas Kinkade Collectors' Society

Dear Collector,

   *Some painters would say that they work with pigment, others with color. I prefer to think that I paint with light. Surely, God paints His creation with light, and that inspires me. I hope you'll agree that there is a radiant quality to my paintings, as if it were lit from within.*

   *That effect is something members of the Thomas Kinkade Collectors' Society especially enjoy. So when I invite you to join us, I'm really urging you to let your light shine. With the help of Collectors' Society members, we'll illuminate a world of beauty and grace this year.*

*Thomas Kinkade*

   By joining the Thomas Kinkade Collectors' Society, you will enter a world of beauty that only Thomas Kinkade can create. Your membership for 1998 will include a very special "Welcome Kit" and members–only benefits to last all year long. For information on how you can join the Thomas Kinkade Collectors' Society visit your local Authorized Dealer or call: 1 . 800 . 544 . 4890

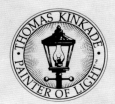

Visit our Website at:
 www.thomaskinkade.com

1998 offers available
January 1, 1998 – December 31, 1998

# Index of Works

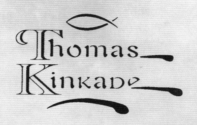